Readings

Worship Feast

100 Readings, Rituals, Prayers, and Guided Meditations

Worship Feast

100 Readings, Rituals, Prayers, and Guided Meditations

Abingdon Press
Nashville

Worship Feast

05 06 07 08 09 10 11 12 13 14—10 9 8 7 6 5 4 3 2 1

MANUFACTURED IN THE UNITED STATES OF AMERICA

COVER DESIGN: KEELY MOORE

Contents

This book is a resource for your church's youth ministry. Feel free to print the prayers, rituals, and meditations in handouts for worship or e-mail the prayers to your students. Use these ideas in your own way to create God encounters for your youth.

Meet the Writer

Jonathon Norman is minister to and with youth at Blakemore and West Nashville United Methodist Churches in Nashville, Tennessee, a member of the International Association for the Study of Youth Ministry, and co-founder/worship leader for The InSearchOf . . . Worship Community, a missional worship group rooted in contemplative styles of worship and prayer. Jonathon has also contributed to two previous volumes of the WORSHIP FEAST series. Besides full-time youth ministry and writing, he is currently working on a Masters of Theology and enjoys spending time at home with his family—his wife Jennifer, Jonas (three-year-old son), and Abby (two-month-old daughter).

Practicing Our Faith

Ritual and Prayer in Youth Ministry

My Journey Is Our Journey

Our lives are made up of practices of one sort or another. If a youth plays soccer, then she commits to practice almost every day so that she knows the rules and can play well. If one of my freshman guys has a band concert, I know he practices his instrument regularly so that he can contribute to the overall performance.

Over time practices shape who we are; they become habits. The same is true for our spiritual lives. Unless we engage ourselves in spiritual practices, we never form habits that form mature Christians.

A few years ago, two things began to happen to me. Thanks to a very good friend of mine, Pastor Michael Williams, I began a journey and discovered the spiritual writings of the desert fathers and mothers of early monasticism. I learned that the monastic methods of prayer and contemplation reached into my heart and drew me very close to God. I had a "Pentecost" experience—the Holy Spirit fell on me anew—and my community was St. Antony of the desert, St. Benedict, and contemporaries like Thomas Merton and Henri Nouwen.

Besides my personal journey, I realized that something was going on in my youth ministry. I had been feeling burned out for several months. One night I decided to lower the lights, play some meditative music, and lead in some centering prayer. I admit that I did this for very selfish reasons: I felt like I needed this time more than the youth did. But after we finished I was surprised to hear that most of the youth thought the experience was very peaceful. Thus began a mutual journey for me as well as my youth group. I learned about spiritual practices and then guided them into what I was learning.

What I discovered from this experience (and continue to) is that our Christian tradition offers many ways to worship God that most modern Christians know little about. I'm glad to see that there is an emerging movement to reclaim ancient practices. I also discovered that Christians can only practice and grow in faith by being connected to a community. Inviting youth to be a part of the body of Christ invites them into a radical and alternative lifestyle called "holy." This "holy" community runs counter to the culture of the consumer-driven world.

The Story-formed Youth Ministry

Christians view the world differently from anyone else; we should. We live out of an incredible story: the story of a God who set apart a people to be God's model to the rest of the world, and

> **When we read Scripture as a community, it is like reading family stories.**

the story of Jesus, God-incarnate, whose life and way of life model to Christians how we are now to live. When we read Scripture as a community, it is like reading family stories. It is these family stories, plus the family traditions (practices), that help shape and inform who we are as this unique culture or community.

Because we live in a fragmented and sometimes violent world, as youth pastors we have to help nurture a community of youth who have an alternative language, an alternative way to handle conflict, and an alternative way of living. This alternative is the Jesus way. This way is informed and passed on to the Christian community not only through participating in spiritual practices together but also through celebrating rituals or rites of passage together. Teens have too few rites of passage to mark and celebrate turning points in their lives. Celebrating rituals in your youth group gives teens the alternative language and status of living in an alternative worldview.

Communal Centered
Christians can't live out their faith in isolation; we must practice our faith in community. We are shaped and formed by learning the unique practices, rituals, and traditions of the church. When practices become habits, hearts are transformed.

The Power of Ritual
Communal rituals or rites can be described as repetitive symbolic and social acts that express and manifest the community's sacred narrative. Thus, for the life of youth ministry, ritual becomes a way to pass along to youth the traditions of the youth group, the local congregation, and the Christian faith. Practicing rituals with youth creates a world for them that has a sacred rhythm.

So much of the time we hear our students talk about their lives being fragmented: parents splitting up, changing schools, changing friends, identity struggles. Rituals break through these situations with a whisper that says: "You are a child of God, beautiful and holy!" They not only bring meaning to our lives but they also bring us together as a family.

Be a Spiritual Director Not a Youth Director

Too often the title "youth director" means something similar to a cruise director—someone who is vocal, witty, charismatic, and ready with fun-filled activities. The problem with this image is that the "director" with all manner of programs and packed schedules causes youth (and youth director!) to miss the ocean and all the surrounding beauty. We miss the horizon and the approaching land with the hope of a better place— a better way of life.

We aren't just leisure directors; we have spiritual responsibilities. Spiritual directors listen to people and help them learn to listen deeply to others and to God. Students are incredibly hungry to listen to and to tell stories. Our role is to help youth learn to listen to one another as they tell their stories and then help them to see how their stories connect with THE story, OUR story, the story of Jesus. That is the role of a spiritual director.

My hope is that this book will introduce you, or further you, along the journey of incorporating spiritual practices into the life of your youth ministry, introducing youth into the most meaningful and truthful story ever: the story of Jesus. May these practices lead to habits, and, over the long haul, add up to a way of life.

Shalom,
Jonathon E. Norman

Section 1
Prayers

Prayers for Times of Suffering

1 God who heals . . . through Jesus you came into the world as healer. . . touching . . . loving . . . restoring those who were hurting. We lift up our friend _____ to you, who is in need of your healing touch, your healing presence, your grace at work.

God who heals . . . guide us as we seek to be a comforting presence. Give us words that are helpful instead of harmful. Teach us what it means to feel empathy and show compassion.

God who heals . . . heal, touch, love, restore, through Christ our Lord, Amen.

2 Rain falls—and there is nothing we can do about it. Rain falls—and for some it's nourishment, for others it's a flood.

The floodwaters have been released, and we pray that you will show us how to turn floodwaters into a source of nourishment. Amen.

3 Jesus, like seasons that come and go, our friend is living through a difficult time. I pray for a springtime breeze in my friend's life—and not a winter ice storm that knocks out the power and leaves everyone stranded. I pray for the peacefulness of the summer air in my friend's season of harsh storms. Amen.

4   A Prayer for a Friend Experiencing the Loss of a Parent

"We don't really understand , Lord." That is what we are feeling right now. You don't seem to be giving any answers. That's OK; we can wait. But our friend—who has lost a parent—can't.

I pray that healing, comfort, and peace will be experienced if answers cannot be revealed in this tragic mystery. Amen.

5   A Prayer Before Serving at a Soup Kitchen

Jesus, you told your followers that when they were serving others who were in need, they were actually serving you. As we gather together to serve a meal and be in ministry with homeless people from various walks of life, help us to see, hear, touch, and experience you through them. Amen.

6   A Prayer to Begin a Youth Meeting

Thank you for each of us gathered here together, Lord. When we gather in this place, all are welcome and loved. Bless this time together. Be with us. Teach us. Let us see you here. Amen.

7   A Prayer to Close a Youth Meeting

Your peace . . .
Your fullness . . .
Your grace, Lord . . .
Surround us . . .
Move around us and through us.
Go with us. Stay with us. Amen.

Prayers for Retreat

8 God of time and space, there won't be much sleep in this place tonight. We give thanks for safe places to come and be together, remembering that some people don't have roofs under which to play, sleep, and relax.
Thank you for this time, eternal Father.
Give us rest, loving Jesus.
Bring us closer to one another, Holy Spirit.
Draw us into your story—your way. Amen.

9 Life has gotten out of hand, and there's just too much going on. We feel out of control, chaotic, and restless—tired but anxious, like a cluttered closet. There's too much going on in our heads.

Lord, it's time to take a time out—to have a team huddle with the Father, Son, and Spirit, to renew, unwind, and refocus. Bless this space that we may experience your goodness and your grace. Amen.

10 **ONE:** For all that seems undone,
For all that seems unresolved,
For all that seems like a burden,
For all that stresses us out.
For the time that is gone.

ALL: Lord, give us peace and rest. Lord, give us rest and peace.

ONE: Strength for the journey,
Mindfulness to clean house . . .
Our inner houses . . .
Our inner sanctuaries . . .
Our souls . . .
Our hearts . . .
And our prayer closets.

ALL: Lord, give us peace and rest. Lord, give us rest and peace.

11 We need a retreat, God—a place for our hearts to listen, a place to take a holy nap. Wrap us up in a prayer quilt and warm our souls, O Lord. Amen.

12 Hustle and Bustle seem to be my first and last names. Rush-hour traffic is my morning coffee. God of sabbath rest, for just a few minutes, change my name to "Cat Nap," and let "Prayer Path" become afternoon tea. Amen.

13 **ONE:** There are seven days in a week, Lord, and there are ten days of activities crammed into that week.
ALL: We need space.

ONE: Space to listen deeply, to be quiet—the kind of quiet where you speak of miracles and beauty. Space to hear music—the kind of music that sings creation into existence.
ALL: We need space.

ONE: Space to feel with emotion—emotion that comes from deep within the heart. Space to breathe deeply—the breath that refreshes like salt water from oceans washing over sun-burned skin.
ALL: God, fill this space with your holy presence.

Prayer Before a Lock-in

14 For all the fun and joy we share when we are together, we give you thanks, O God. We remember and pray for those who suffer from depression or loneliness and for those who feel they don't belong.

This place, this space, this group is a place of belonging and blessing. Thank you, Lord, for this time set apart to spend together. Amen.

Prayers for Exam Times

15 Gracious and loving God, it's time for semester tests and exams. Be present in our thoughts and minds. Keep us in the moment, focused, and clear. Amen.

16 Good Teacher Jesus, please be with all teachers and professors giving exams and end-of-semester tests, as well as all students who are taking exams. All that you give is good, and all that is good comes from you.

> We give you thanks for the ability to learn.
> We give you thanks for knowledge and wisdom.
> We give you thanks for a community of adults
>   whose passion is to pass along knowledge.
> We give you thanks for peers and friends who help
>   to create a community at our school.
> As we gather in the coming days to take exams,
> help us to remember all that we have learned throughout
> the semester. Amen.

17 Loving God, thank you that we don't have to take a test to earn your love. You love us for who we are. Help us find confidence in our belovedness and know that we can do all things in Christ our strength. Give us clarity and patience. Amen.

18 God of hope, It is not likely that I will pass this exam. I have not studied, and I have not applied myself during this semester. This exam will reflect my lack of dedication. You promise that nothing will separate us from your love. I realize that I must face the consequences of possibly failing this exam, but I pray that your grace will abound despite the circumstances. Help me to experience your presence today and every day. Amen.

19 A Prayer for Discernment

The prayer on the following pages is an ancient form of prayer used to guide Christians in making decisions. It can be applied to most any life decision and has been adapted from an ancient monastic prayer model called the "Ignatian Prayer."

BEGINNING THE PRAYER

Spend a moment telling God the decision that you are contemplating.

Completely visualize the issues involved in making this decision. When you feel ready, pray this prayer:

I come before you, God, to ask your help in a hard decision that I'm facing. Please bring me clarity and peace as I pray. Amen.

(Spend some time in silence, clearing your mind and stilling your inner noise.)

STEP 1: CONSIDER THE CHOICES

Think through the decision in a prayerful manner by considering all the different choices you could make. Also consider each possible consequence of the choices. It may be helpful to record your thoughts in a journal.

STEP 2: ADVICE

If you were to ask advice from a friend concerning this decision, who would that friend be? Visualize that friend and imagine what his or her advice might be. Record the response in your journal.

STEP 3: CHAT WITH GOD

Now it's time to bring your decision before the Lord. Think about the choices you were considering originally, the advice that you imagined your friend giving, and then ask God about it. Don't worry about receiving a solid, straightforward answer. Instead, listen for a "heart nudge" that gives you peace of mind.

STEP 4: SLEEP ON IT

Don't make any choices concerning this decision for at least two days. You may want to call your friend, discuss the matter, or journal some more. Also spend some time in silence, listening for God's direction.

STEP 5: NOW YOU'RE READY

Once you have worked through this "prayerful process," you are ready to take action. This process doesn't necessarily guarantee that you have made the best decision, but it is a "practice" in bringing God into your decision-making process. If you feel that you are not ready to act, or that the choice you are leaning towards is still not the right choice, start at the beginning and work through the discernment process again.

Prayers for New Beginnings

20 **ONE:** It's a new school year, Lord. I've changed a lot since last year, but I know I still have a ways to go. I'm looking forward to a fresh start.

ALL: I pray for my old friends.

ONE: Help them to see that although I've changed things about myself, I still want their friendship and that I am still me.

ALL: I pray for my teachers.

ONE: I pray that they will have open minds about me and will trash my reputation as "old news."

ALL: I pray for strength.

ONE: I'm excited about what this year will bring, but I'm also nervous that I'll fall back into my old ways. I know that you are faithful and that you promise to walk with your children. I want to be as faithful to you, myself, and others as you are to me.

ALL: Through Christ our Lord we pray.

21 I woke up this morning and it was a brand new day. Thank you, Lord. I never want to re-live yesterday. A new day can be like your grace—a new start, a new beginning.

I woke up this morning and it was a brand new day. Thank you, Lord. May your grace encompass my whole being so that I may fully appreciate this new start—this brand new day. Amen.

Prayers for Interfaith Experiences

22 Through Jesus Christ there is no Jew or Greek. God, we live a unique story of your love through Christ Jesus. But there are other stories and other traditions. Help us to understand and appreciate what other traditions add to the world. Jews, Muslims, Buddhists, Hindus, and others are our brothers and sisters. But you, Lord Jesus, are our way. Amen.

23 God of peace, this world has experienced too much violence because of religion. We have been intolerant, claiming "the only way" to you. Today there is too much silence and fear and not enough sharing and love. God of peace, help us to be architects of large, comfortable couches where people of all faith traditions can come tell their stories and experience your love. Amen.

Prayers for Families

24 Prayer for When You're Away From Family

Lord, I feel a long way from my family. Even though I don't always want to admit it, at this time I really miss them. I pray that your presence will be with them—just as your presence with me helps me feel close to them when we are separated. Keep them safe and bring us together again soon. Amen.

25 A Prayer for Conflict Resolution

Lord, I'm afraid our family is going to bed angry tonight. How can I be an instrument of your peace in this household? I want to, but the desire for peace and resolution has to go both ways—someone willing to offer it and someone willing to accept it. I pray that you will open a way for healing and reconciliation in this conflict. Amen.

26 A Prayer for Vacation

Lord, family vacations sometimes end up feeling more like cruel and unusual punishment rather than the anticipated rest and relaxation. We pray that this vacation will be a time to relax, meet one another's needs, and draw closer as a family. Help us to enjoy one another and to make new and special memories. Amen.

27 A Prayer for Youth Whose Parents Are Divorcing

Christ Jesus, I feel really alone. I don't know how to tell my parents how I feel about their divorce without yelling or crying. I'd rather just stay in my bedroom and listen to music. Can you heal this situation?

Is there anyone else out there who feels this way?

Is anyone listening?

Lord, send me someone I can talk to . . .

Lord, send me someone who will listen . . .

Let me hear the words I need to hear . . .

Let me hear your Word.

Please bring some sense of peace to this turmoil. Amen.

Prayers for Justice

28 Jesus, you call those who follow you to look and act different from the rest of the world. You call us to be a just and loving culture. You call us to live in a way that shows we follow these two rules: "Love God" and "Love your neighbor." Help us to live a life of love so that those who are watching will see you and want to follow also. Amen.

29 **ONE:** People all over the world live in poverty while we live in such a wealthy nation. I don't understand why it's this way, Lord.

ALL: Lord, I wish it were different and so do you.

ONE: I think of children who don't have all that they need to survive and thrive in this world: medical attention, shelter, nourishment, clothing, attention, and touch—things that most of us take for granted.

ALL: Lord, I wish it were different and so do you.

ONE: Lord, I think of people who live in run-down neighborhoods because they don't have the money or power to change things. Those with power and resources have left and built new neighborhoods.

ALL: Lord, I wish it were different and so do you.

ONE: Lord, we can make a difference by choosing justice over self, choosing to live in a way that assures all your children have what they need. We can live in a way that helps the world look more the way you and I both wish it would.

ALL: Lord, help us to live so that your dreams come true.

Prayers for New Year's Eve

30 Mysterious New Beginning, in this hour nothing else matters except that I come before you.

Mysterious Healer, in this moment nothing else matters except that you forgive my past mistakes.

Mysterious Maker, in this moment nothing else matters except that you don't give up on your children. Please continue to make us whole.

Holy Mystery, like the fragrance of incense, fill my insides with flowering grace. Fill me with your Spirit that I may love others. Fill me with your holiness that I may be a blessing to others.

Holy Mystery, surround me with those who love the way you love. Surround me with grace to start fresh. Amen.

31 It is late. It is dark. The past and the future have converged. This new year offers opportunity and hope—a fresh new start.

Surround us, Lord—above and below us,
To our right and to our left, Lord . . .
All around us, Lord.

As we remember the past year and the narrative of our lives, we realize we've changed. As we look ahead to the new year and the unfolding story of our lives, we are confident that you will walk alongside us through life's experiences. Amen.

32 It is no surprise that this night has rolled around again. There's nothing magical or extraordinary about midnight. But somehow, with the coming of a new year, there is hope that things can change . . .
 . . . for the world,
 . . . for those who suffer,
 . . . for friends who struggle,
 . . . for the conflicts,
 . . . for the aspects of my life that I wish were different.

Yet with this night comes much to celebrate in life . . .
 . . . for beauty,
 . . . for those who bring joy to me,
 . . . for those who bring peace and healing,
 . . . for those areas of my life in which I've grown during the past year.

For the joy and the sorrow, thanks is given to you, Holy Mystery. For through both, we continue to grow. Amen.

Prayers for Peace

33 Jesus, two thousand years ago you showed us a way to live without violence. Why can't your children get along? When will your kingdom come? How long will we continue to do harm to one another? Help all Christians to live life in a way that shows the world how to live. Amen.

34 No more tanks . . .
No more machine guns . . .
No more generals . . .
No more war, we pray.

No more grenades . . .
No more mines . . .
No more children dying for the powerful . . .
No more war, we pray.

Let's all sit and talk.
Let's all play and dance.
Let's all listen to one another's stories.
Peace will come, this we pray.

Let's host parties where all are invited.
Let's take time outs when we get angry.
Let's create a world where war is just a card game that
  two friends play late at night when there's nothing
  else to do.
Peace will come, this we pray.

35 Lord, my home feels like a war zone. No one is
getting along, no one is talking, and I feel caught
in the middle. I hear about war abroad and countries
fighting, but I'd settle for a little "good will"
in my home right now. Please, bring peace;
come quickly, Lord. Amen.

36 There is so much noise inside my head that I can't focus on any one thing. I hear the sounds of my life—my busy, hurried, frantic life. Holy God, help me to stop and rest and to feel your peace. Amen.

Prayers for Relationships

37 Great God of love, all loving relationships are visible symbols of your love. You are the wellspring of our love. Let us be vessels of your perfect love. May our relationships grow in a way that shows others what healthy, loving relationships look like. Strengthen us to love as you love. Amen.

38 God, why can't anyone understand what I'm going through? I try to talk to my parents, but it's like talking to a wall (or maybe talking to me is like talking to a wall)—that's how I feel right now—like a cracked wall that needs a little patching. I just want someone to say, "I love you."

Lord, your grace is the patchwork that heals. I pray that you would mend the cracked walls that are separating me from my parents. Amen.

39 God, you created us to be in relationship with you and with one another. Relationships are hard. We don't want to be fake, but sometimes we just don't like a person and we need your love to pierce through our feelings and cause us to show love. Help us be real and be loving. Amen.

40 A Prayer for Youth Going Through a Breakup

Jesus, I am so confused. I really thought I was in love. Maybe I still am. I'm not sure what I feel, but I know that my heart is broken. Please bring me clarity of mind and wholeness of heart. Give me peace instead of the confusion I'm experiencing. Amen.

(Sit and be still. Focus on your breathing and clear your mind. Listen for God in the silence, paying close attention to passing thoughts and the different emotions that you feel. Continue to ask God for clarity and discernment concerning the direction of the relationship.)

41 A Prayer for the Environment

Lord of Creation, you call us, your children, to care for all that you have created. We pray for those animals and plants that are now extinct because of our lack of concern. We pray for those animals and plants that are close to extinction. Your concern and love for them goes unnoticed by your people.

Forgive our silence. Give us VOICES that sing a new song, speak a new language, and tell stories of your love for creation. And give us HANDS that care for your creation. Amen.

Prayers for the Evening

42 It was at night, Lord Jesus, that you told stories to your friends around a fire. Come tell us stories now at the close of the day.

It was at night, Lord Jesus, when you washed the feet of friends you loved. Come and wash us now, Lord, so that the wounds of the day may heal with your touch.

It was at night, Lord Jesus, that you shared a meal of bread and wine with those to whom you were closest. Come and share your love with your friends again.

It was at night, Lord Jesus, that you lay silent in a tomb—but with morning came new life, light out of darkness. Go with us now into the night and wake with us tomorrow. Amen.

43 **A Candlelight Prayer**
You will need three candles for this prayer.

We light a candle for you, our God and Creator, for you are like a parent who enjoys us, who is frustrated by us, who mourns over us, who loves us, and who is proud of us. We light a candle to remind us that the light of your love and presence goes with us into the night.
(*Light candle 1.*).

We light a candle for you, Jesus the Son, for you are like a big brother who gave us an example of how to live together, how to love, how to learn from others, how to live in peace in the midst of violence, how to choose life over death. We light a candle to remind us that the light of your love and presence goes with us into the night. (*Light candle 2.*)

We light a candle for you, God the Spirit, for you are like wind that blows leaves around in the fall. Somehow, in the most mysterious way, your people have come together through you as the body of Christ. It is through you that we are able to be a light to others, to be a light that lights up a dark world. We light a candle to remind us that the light of your love and presence goes with us into the night.
(*Light candle 3.*)

We light three candles tonight for Creator, Son, and Spirit—three in one; for wholeness, perfect grace, mercy, and hope, we give you thanks. Amen.

Prayers for the Rhythm of Faith

44 Advent
Long-expected Jesus, like watching for shooting stars in a field on a cool, clear night, we anticipate your coming. As we seek you, help us also to excite others to watch for your coming. Amen.

45 Christmas

Holy baby Jesus, you came bringing the most extraordinary gift anyone could imagine—a way for the world to live together—in love with one another and with God. This Christmas we thank you for the gift of your Son, Jesus Christ, and our friends, family, and community—where this love can be lived out. Amen.

46 Epiphany

Gifted One, through the power of your Spirit we each come before you with gifts. We don't bring expensive or extravagant gifts; instead we bring our very lives. Help us to use the gifts and talents you have given us to bless others. In the name of the Father, Son, and Spirit. Amen.

47 Lent

Jesus, just as you ventured into the wilderness to face alienation and temptation, so we travel to a desert place in our souls to listen for God's call in our lives. Travel alongside us and speak a word that guides us into a greater understanding of your will for our lives. Amen.

48 Good Friday

Sometimes you feel so far away, God, that it seems as if you don't exist. When I feel this way I am so easily distracted from seeking your will. Don't let me stray too far God. Sometimes it is easier to stray than to seek. Please hold on to me. Amen.

49 Easter

Roll away my confusion, Lord, like the stone that was rolled away from the tomb. I want to hear you ask, "Who is it that you seek?" You are a mystery that words cannot quite express, but I pray that you would give me words to express the love I have for you. Amen.

50 Pentecost

Come, Holy Spirit, stir up the winds of peace, hope, love, and joy. Bring your children together in ways that we've never imagined or believed possible. Send your spirit of unity upon the body of Christ and let us be as one. Amen.

51 A Prayer for Those Who Persecute You

How can we love when we feel so hurt? How can we see past our pain? You tell us to love our enemies—and that sounds good on paper—but right this second we need more practical advice.

Do you really call us to love, right now, right this second? We're not sure that we can.

How do we love those who persecute us? Lord, be our strength when we have none. Amen.

Prayers to Start the Morning

52 In the beginning, before your breath
created life, you imagined . . .
You spoke and your words became living things.
You imagined and you created.

In the beginning, before there was light, the
world was in darkness.
But you spoke, and the sun, the stars, and the moon
came into being.

Today we awake from another night's sleep—breathing
the air that comes from your Spirit.
Today we join you for another day of enjoying life.
We celebrate the blessings of the earth.

Today help us to be co-creators with you, O Lord,
responding to the needs of others around us just as you
respond to our needs. Amen.

53 **This morning is a new day . . .**
. . . of work. Lord, give me strong hands and a
focused mind.

. . . of study. Lord, open my mind to new thoughts
and ideas.

. . . of play. Lord, teach us, your children, to play
well together.

. . . of war. Lord, teach us a different way.

. . . of peace. Lord, be with the few who follow.

. . . of hunger. Lord, please fill the mouths of those with empty bellies and teach us to share.

. . . of abuse. Lord, help us stand up for the victims and heal their hurts.

. . . of tenderness. Lord, bring us healing and help us to offer healing to others.

. . . of alienation. Lord, help us to find our way home.

. . . of community. Lord, help us to open our doors and be welcoming to everyone. Amen.

54 Yesterday's scars were laid to rest last night. Today we awake with your love on our minds. Thank you, O wise Creator, for knowing that what we needed was a good night's sleep. Rest brings a fresh outlook.

This morning is a new day, a new day to live life the way you call us to live. Help us to hear your voice, Lord, and be obedient to your call. Amen.

55 *Prayers of God's Goodness*

Lord, your love is a land without borders. All are welcome and all are invited to stay. Once your love is found, everything else takes care of itself. Forgive us for putting up fences around your love. Help us to open the floodgates of your grace. Amen.

56 In the beginning you walked through the garden with Adam and Eve—
Because you enjoy being with your children.

When you saw your people suffering in Egypt, you walked your children to safety through a parted Red Sea—
Because you care for your children.

When your people strayed, you sent them into exile, but you never gave up nor abandoned them—
Because you are faithful to your children.

When there was no other way to reach us, you came to us as Jesus, showing how deeply you love, loving even as you were crucified—
Because your love knows no boundaries.

Even today your love remains the same as it was in the beginning. You continue to walk alongside your people. You continue to care for your children. You are faithful. How grateful we are, O God, for this never-ending love. Amen.

57 Lord, we pray for those we know and those we don't—those who feel like they are outsiders. Our doors are open, Lord. We pray that we who are comfortable and accepted will not be blinded by our comfort and exclude those around us. As insiders looking out, let us not only look but also reach out to others. Amen.

Prayers for Times of Joy

58 Breathing in life . . .
Breathing out life . . .
Breathing in joy. . .
Breathing out peace.

Living in the present tense . . .
Living in the moment . . .
Appreciating life . . .
I appreciate you, Holy Maker.

Tasting joy . . .
Feeling joy . . .
Hearing joy . . .
Touching joy . . .
Smelling joy . . .

All around me the joy of life exists.

Inhaling blessings from all around,
Exhaling blessings to others,
Joy is taken in, loved, and appreciated.
Love is spread all around, shared like a meal with
strangers and friends.

For this we give thanks, O Lord. Amen.

59 Life is good right now. I wish I could live in this moment forever, always feeling this joy in my heart—like sunshine after rain, or like waking up for school and finding out it's a snow day. I am so thankful. If I had never lived a bad day, then I wouldn't know what a day filled with joy feels like. So today I give you thanks for the good and bad days—and I pray that I will live this moment to the fullest. Amen.

60 I give you thanks for the people who bring me joy. (*Name those people.*)

I give you thanks for the recent experiences that have brought me happiness. (*Name those experiences.*)

Sometimes I fail to see that you, God, are present in the daily activities and relationships of my life. For the mystery of your presence, I am thankful. Amen.

I Woke Up!

61 ONE: I woke up this morning.
ALL: **What a blessing!**

ONE: I am in good health.
ALL: **What a blessing!**

ONE: All around me I see symbols of God's love.
ALL: **What a blessing!**

62   Living in Today's World

VOICE 1: I look at the world and I hurt. I hurt for those who suffer; I hurt for those who are victims of genocide; O Lord, I hurt.

VOICE 2: I look at the faces around me and I hurt. I hurt for homeless teenagers on the streets. I hurt for children whose homes have been bombed and whose parents have been lost. O Lord, I hurt.

ALL: O Lord, heal the hurt that encompasses the earth.

63   Facing the Injustice of the World

(Allow a brief time for participants to name those issues of injustice for which they are concerned.)

VOICE: Forgive us, Holy God, for watching the news and not speaking up.

ALL: Give us strength to raise up words to our leaders so that they will hear our voices. Give us voices that speak truth in the midst of the hurt and confusion.

64   A Prayer for Peace

Voice 1: Jesus came to overcome evil through violence!
All: No, he did not!

Voice 1: Well, Jesus said to take all you can from whomever you can by any means that you can!
All: No, he did not!

Voice 1: Didn't Jesus say if someone strikes you to strike him back?
All: Not quite.

Voice 2: Jesus came to overcome evil with peace. He even went to the cross.
All: That's right.

Voice 2: Jesus said that to follow him you must deny yourself and take up a cross.
All: The way of Christ is the way of peace.

Voice 2: Jesus said that if someone strikes you, you should turn your other cheek and show him your strength through love.
All: Love is stronger than evil.

65 A Reading for Beginning or Ending a Mission Trip

LEADER: I am fragile . . . broken . . . and in need of an overhaul, some rest, and some "TLC."
ALL: Where love is . . .
   God is.

LEADER: I've been beaten down by life, pushed out of the way, and silenced. I've lost hope . . .
Where do I go for a little hope?
ALL: We go in love, so wherever we go . . .
   There will be love.

LEADER: I'm a real person with thoughts, ideas, life experiences, stories to tell, tears to cry, and burdens to carry.
ALL: So wherever we go . . .
   God will be present.

LEADER: When you served one of the least in life, you served me.
ALL: God is present in those we serve in love.

ALL: Christ is present in those we serve in love. God is present in those we serve in love.

66 A Reading for Advent

VOICE 1: I have a picture of you in my head.
ALL: Will we recognize you when you come?

VOICE 2: His light burns bright and illuminates the way.
ALL: The way to love.

VOICE 1: I have a picture of you in my head.
ALL: Will we recognize you when you come?

VOICE 3: His feet walk the path, the path that leads the way.
ALL: The way to peace.

Voice 1: I have a picture of you in my head.
ALL: Will we recognize you when you come?

VOICE 4: His voice calls us even today, calls us to follow the way.
ALL: The way to life.

VOICE 1: I have a picture of you in my head, Jesus.

VOICE 2: And you look like love.

VOICE 3: And you look like peace.

VOICE 4: And you look like life flowing.

ALL: We have a picture of you in our heads, Jesus. And even if we don't recognize you when you come, you will recognize us.

67　A Table Blessing

One: God's love is huge.
All: We feast at God's heavenly banquet.

One: God takes care of God's own.
All: We feast at God's heavenly banquet.

One: God fills our hungry souls.
All: We feast at God's heavenly banquet.

One: God fills our hungry bellies.
All: We feast at God's heavenly banquet.

One: God is good.
All: All the time!

One: All the time . . .
All: God is good!

Section 2
Rituals

68 A Ritual for Closing a Youth Gathering

THE BIG PICTURE

Never underestimate simplicity and touch as you build rituals. My youth group practiced a ritual to close youth group meetings even before I arrived. This ritual is not new, but I've included it because it is tradition. The repetition of spiritual practices and the handing down of "traditions" is the story of our faith being passed from one generation to the next. So in developing a closing ritual for your youth group, choose one that will last.

THE RITUAL

Invite youth to stand in a circle and join hands, crossing right arms over left. Everyone's right hand should hold a partner's left hand and everyone's left hand should hold the other partner's right hand. Together everyone says this blessing aloud:

The Lord bless you and keep you;
The Lord make his face to shine upon you
and be gracious to you;
The Lord lift up his countenance upon you
and give you peace. Amen.

(Numbers 6:24-26)

As the group members say "Amen," they should turn around and twist their arms to face outside the circle, symbolizing the group as it goes out into the world.

69 A Ritual for the Beginning of a Youth Gathering

THE BIG PICTURE

Although teenagers enjoy adventure and experiencing new and different things, a part of them also needs routine. A ritual for beginning a youth gathering is an excellent way to establish routine and consistency for your youth. There are many traditions and rituals used by youth groups to open or close their meetings, so if you do not have a tradition, I invite you to create one.

GETTING STARTED

Use small taper candles or tea light candles (one per youth and leader). If you use taper candles, make sure you provide something to catch dripping wax.

THE RITUAL

Once students have assembled, ask them to sit in a circle, then give a candle to each youth. Begin by telling one person to light a candle and state the two most important events of his or her week. When this person is finished, she or he should light the next person's candle and extinguish her or his own. Continue the process until everyone around the circle has spoken.

70 A Ritual for Celebrating a Student Getting a Driver's License

THE BIG PICTURE

Obtaining a driver's license is a monumental rite of passage in the life of a teenager. As the church, we should seek God's blessings on the ordinary parts of our lives, thus making them sacred. I cannot think of a place where God's blessing is more necessary than on the streets where teenagers drive. Students need to be reminded that their faith is lived out even while driving a car—and that God is concerned with how we treat our neighbors on the road and how we care for ourselves and those we are transporting.

GETTING STARTED

In my church we give a special key chain to youth when they receive their driver's licenses. The key chain is a visual reminder that they practice their faith while on the road. Invite youth to bring their driver's license with them to the ritual. Hold this ritual once or twice a year.

THE RITUAL

Ask all youth who have recently received their driver's licenses to sit at the front of the group. Create a worship altar using one candle for each person being recognized, each person's license, and the key chains. Place the altar behind where the students sit.

Opening Words: "Our faith as Christians is lived out in the day-to-day experiences of our lives. One of the most ordinary but exciting parts of teenage life is getting a driver's license. This license brings us one step closer to independence, freedom, and the outside world. But with freedom comes responsibility and a respect for all of life.

"As you move into this new and mobile stage of life, remember you have a responsibility to your family, church, friends, and those in need. Also remember that God is present wherever you are—no matter how distant or close you may *feel* to God."

Invite each youth to the altar, one at a time, and call out his or her name. Invite each to light a candle and take his or her license and a key chain. After students have lit candles and picked up their licenses and key chains, close with the following prayer:

Almighty God, your love knows no boundaries.
Your love goes with us throughout our lives,
no matter the road we travel. Be with (say each
student's name) as (he or she) begins another part of
life's journey. Help (him or her) to see that
you are in the passenger seat and will never
leave (his or her) side. Amen.

71 A Ritual for the Journey Through Lent

THE BIG PICTURE

Lent is a season of forty days (not including Sundays) that begins on Ash Wednesday and ends the Saturday before Easter. Historically, Lent began as a period of fasting and preparation for baptism but evolved into a time for penance by all Christians. Lent is a wonderful time for youth to explore Christian practices such as fasting or prayer.

GETTING STARTED

In this ritual youth will be walking a prayer path that leads them through a Lent experience. Along the path there will be stations at which the youth may stop to reflect and pray. At the final station, youth will be invited to commit to a specific spiritual practice during Lent, such as fasting or daily prayer. Items needed for the stations are as follows:

Station 1: a small bowl with ashes
Station 2: several mirrors, smooth stones, markers
Station 3: pitcher of water, small cups
Station 4: large sheet of paper with a cross drawn in the center, markers, index cards, pens

Create a handout for each station using the Scriptures, explanations, and meditations.

THE RITUAL

Begin by inviting youth to remove their shoes and socks and to sit in silence. Once they feel ready, invite them to journey through the stations and use the handouts as prayer guides.

STATION 1: ASHES

"God commanded the Man, 'You can eat from any tree in the garden, except from the Tree-of-Knowledge-of-Good-and-Evil. Don't eat from it. The moment you eat from that tree, you're dead." (Genesis 2:16-17, *THE MESSAGE*)

Lent is a journey that takes us into the desert with Jesus and invites us to abandon our normal routines of life, reflecting on our inner most being. Like Jesus, and all of humanity since the beginning of time, we are tempted. When we enter the desert with Jesus, we become more aware of the temptations that distance us from God.

Meditation

Imagine yourself entering the desert with Jesus.
What does it feel like?
What parts of your life do you bring with you?
What do you need to leave behind?

As you begin this journey, dip your finger into the ashes and place a mark of ashes on your forehead, for like Adam at the beginning of time, you are human and share in the same journey that all have faced before you and will face after.

STATION 2: LIVING STONES

"Directed by God, the whole company of Israel moved on by stages from the Wilderness of Sin. . . . There wasn't a drop of water for the people to drink. . . . The people were thirsty for water there. They complained to Moses, 'Why did you take us from Egypt and drag us out here with our children and animals to die of thirst?' God said to Moses, 'Go on out ahead of the people, taking with you some of the elders of Israel. Take the staff you used to strike the Nile. And go. I'm going to be present before you there on the rock at Horeb. You are to strike the rock. Water will gush out of it and the people will drink." (Exodus 17:1-3, 5-6 *THE MESSAGE*)

When we wander into the wilderness, we often find ourselves alone—and sometimes desperate. We don't feel like we can go forward. Where is God in the midst of this desperation?

Meditation
Like the ancient Israelites,
when we wander through the desert, we are lost.
But we know that God provides when we are in need.
Choose one of the rocks and hold it in your hand.
Think about the ways that God provides for your needs
even when you cannot see. Write a word on your rock
that describes who God is to you. Take your rock with
you on your journey.

STATION 3: LIVING WATER.

"You are to strike the rock. Water will gush out of it and the people will drink." (Exodus 17:6, *THE MESSAGE*)

Deserts are known for being dry, barren, and dead. As Jesus was being led away from the garden of Gethsemane on the night of his arrest, he probably felt as though he had once again entered the wilderness—abandoned, alone, frightened, and weak.

But Jesus lived his life knowing that God provides for those who follow. No matter how far we feel from God, we live with the assurance that God can take all the world's problems and hurts and turn them into something to celebrate.

Meditation

Reflect upon those things that cause you to struggle or that cause you to feel distant from God or others.
Maybe you should focus on a relationship that needs healing. Sit in silence and imagine God's healing love surrounding your struggles.

When you feel ready, pour a cup of God's "living water" and have a drink—symbolizing God's love that provides grace in the midst of your struggles.

STATION 4: THE CROSS FROM A DISTANCE

"From noon to three, the whole earth was dark. Around mid-afternoon Jesus groaned out of the depths, crying loudly, *'Eli, Eli, lama sabachtahni?'* which means, 'My God, my God, why have you abandoned me?'" (Matthew 27:45-46, *THE MESSAGE*)

Surely the disciples felt desperate. They gave up everything to follow Jesus: good jobs, spouses, family, homes, EVERYTHING. Now the one for whom they sacrificed it all was gone. Can you imagine the disciples' desperation?

Meditation

Look at the cross. Imagine that you are one of Jesus'
disciples and are witnessing his crucifixion from a
distance, perhaps on a hillside away from where
all the people are gathered.
How do you feel as you watch?
What are you thinking?
Write a word on the paper that describes how
you feel as you witness Jesus' death.

Now imagine that Jesus is inviting you to follow him
during the next forty days of Lent.
What will you give up (or take on) in order to follow him?
Using an index card, write a letter to God explaining
what you will give up or focus on during Lent
to deepen your walk with God.

72 A Ritual for When One of Your Youth Moves Away

THE BIG PICTURE

Change is a constant part of life in youth ministry. By nature youth groups are fluid, and students come and go with each passing year. Rituals to mark the end of a student's participation in the life of the youth group is meaningful for both the student leaving and the students saying goodbye. This ritual is appropriate when a student is moving away, either unexpectedly (such as a parent's job relocation), or because he or she is entering the next phase of life after graduation.

GETTING STARTED

Obtain permission from the governing body of your church before you use this idea. Choose a place on your church property to create a memory garden. The idea is to plant a tree or flower every time someone leaves the youth group. In addition to plants or seeds, you will also need small cups of water (one for each student in the youth group).

The plants and flowers will serve as reminders that those youth who have moved on continue to be remembered as a special part of the community.

THE RITUAL

Invite all the youth into the garden. Ask the youth who is moving to plant the seeds or tree or flower. When he or she is finished, say: "Just as these plants provide enrichment to the soil and add beauty to this space, you have enriched the life of our youth group and made it beautiful. May the prayers and hopes of this youth group travel with you wherever you go."

Next, give out the cups and tell youth to pour the water over the plant or seeds. As they do so, invite them to say a blessing for the student leaving, such as, "(*Say student's name*), may God bring you _____." Close with a huge group hug, asking the student(s) who are leaving to stand in the middle.

73   A Ritual for Passing Peace

THE BIG PICTURE

"Passing of the Peace" is an element of worship in many churches. It can also be an effective ritual for allowing youth to experience compassion in the context of worship.

Shalom is a Hebrew word meaning peace or God's wholeness in the world. So when we offer one another "Shalom," we aren't just offering peace to someone but also the grace and love of Christ that touches the mind, body, and heart. "Shalom Aleichem" is a traditional Hebrew greeting that means "May God's peace be upon you."

GETTING STARTED

Tell youth the meaning of "Shalom Aleichem" and explain that when we greet one another with this phrase we are connecting with the ancient roots of our heritage in Judaism, and we are sharing peace for the mind, body, and soul of all living creatures. Also remind them that this peace comes from living the way God desires, and it is a peace that changes us mentally, physically, and spiritually.

THE RITUAL

When we offer God's shalom to one another, as a youth group we are agreeing to live together the way God expects and as a model to other people. So, to offer God's shalom to one another, we extend our arms and hands with our palms face up. Next, cup your hands under someone's hands (you are holding his or her hands, face up, in yours). This gesture symbolizes that as a community we hold each other in love. Now look at that person and say, "Shalom Aleichem." Then trade hand positions and repeat the blessing.

74 A Ritual for a Rainy Day

THE BIG PICTURE

One reason for observing rituals is that they allow us to discover sacredness in the ordinary aspects of our lives. This ritual provides an opportunity to turn rain—which is normally a bummer, but still God's gift—into a holy moment.

GETTING STARTED

Although you can do this at any time during the year, I live in the southeast part of the United States, and there's no way that I'm doing this ritual in the winter. So with that said, springtime is probably the best time for a "Rainy Day Ritual." You will need strips of paper, watercolor paints, and a rainy day.

THE RITUAL

While you are in a covered area, invite youth to name situations in their lives that give them the "blahs." Hand out strips of paper and watercolor paints and ask youth to paint or write their "blahs" on the paper strips.

After a few minutes, explain to youth that they will be taking their "blahs" outside. (If they wish, students may remove their socks and shoes to keep them from getting wet while they are outside in the rain.)

Once the group is outside, ask them to read aloud their "blahs" (one at a time), then to hold their papers out in the rain, allowing it to smear the words or pictures. Close with the following reading:

LEADER: Lord, like water that falls from the sky, you come to us. In the most healing ways, like rain, you renew and cleanse everything you touch.

EVERYONE: You take the blahs away.

LEADER: Like rain, your grace falls on everyone, showing no partiality.

EVERYONE: You take the blahs away.

LEADER: Like rain, your love takes the withered up and dry—and refreshes and brings new life.

EVERYONE: You take the blahs away.

LEADER: O Lord, take away the blahs on this rainy day. Show us your love in only your way.

EVERYONE: You take the blahs away.

75 A Ritual for Saying Good-bye to a Youth Leader

THE BIG PICTURE

Like all close relationships, losing a youth pastor can be extremely difficult for a youth group, as well as the youth leader who is leaving. A goodbye ritual can help provide closure and healing. Also, I am convinced that each group has a unique story to tell—a story that sets it apart from other youth groups. Participating in this ritual helps the students to see themselves as unique, set apart, and special, while symbolizing that the story will go on, even after the current youth leader leaves.

GETTING STARTED

For this ritual you will need a strip of white fabric and fabric paint. Use the fabric to create a stole, the symbol for being called by God. During a planned fellowship time, youth and youth leaders will tell unique youth-group stories and affirm the characteristics that set it apart from other youth groups.

THE RITUAL

Plan an entire evening for storytelling. Ask the youth and youth leaders to recall their most memorable stories while participating in the youth group. Once the ball gets rolling, you may have trouble slowing it down. Everyone loves to tell personal stories.

Next, explain to the group that together you are going to create a youth group stole to pass along to the new youth director. The stole should represent the identity of the youth group. Students can write words on the stole that describe their group or they can draw pictures and symbols. You may want to leave blank space on the stole so that the group can add to the stole whenever there is a change in leadership.

After the youth group has finished decorating the stole, spend some time talking about what each word or picture represents. Then display the stole prominently in the meeting room until the new youth pastor arrives to receive it.

76 A Ritual for Welcoming a New Youth Leader

THE BIG PICTURE
I developed this ritual when I left the position of youth pastor at my local church. It was an interesting situation because I remained a member of the church. Because I had not left the congregation nor the community, we had a "Passing of the Mantle" ceremony when the new youth pastor arrived. It wasn't a formal gathering, just a time for youth and youth leaders to gather and tell about the history and traditions of the youth group.

GETTING STARTED

You will need either the stole that you created in "A Ritual for Saying Goodbye to a Youth Leader" or another item that symbolizes the youth group's character. In a perfect youth ministry world, it would be appropriate to include both the previous youth pastor and the new youth pastor—one to pass the mantle and one to receive it. The act of transferring the stole is a powerful visual of continuity.

THE RITUAL

Invite youth and parents, youth workers, former youth pastor, new youth pastor, and senior minister to attend. (You may also want to extend this invitation to other people in the congregation.)

In this ritual youth tell about meaningful youth group experiences. The time is not meant to be a "pat on the back" for the former youth leader; instead it is a time for the group to tell its unique story to the new youth pastor.

Once everyone who wishes has participated, the former youth director should give the leadership "mantle" to the new youth director. Then invite everyone to say this blessing:

Gracious God, we are thankful for (insert name of my youth leader) and all the gifts (he or she) brings to our youth group.
Watch over (him or her), guide (insert name) in your ways, and continue to guide us and help us to be faithful to your calling. Amen.

77   A Ritual for Prayer-like Smoke Signals

THE BIG PICTURE

This ritual invites youth to think about the gifts God has given them and how they can use those gifts in the youth group, in church, or for the good of others.

GETTING STARTED

You need a large metal bowl (or some sort of cauldron), index cards, pens, a lighter, and some ambient or meditative background music.

THE RITUAL

Invite youth to think about their talents and how they are presently using them. Tell them to list their talents on one side of an index card. Then ask, "In what ways do you see these talents as gifts from God?" or "In what ways can these talents or gifts be used for God's good in the world?"

Spend some time discussing the questions. Then explain that, as a group, you will spend time in prayer and reflect on ways to use our talents for God.

When students are finished, have them offer their cards to God as burnt offerings, symbolizing the promises they have made to God to use their talents for good. Close by reading aloud Acts 2:1-4.

78 A Ritual for Welcoming New Youth into the Group

THE BIG PICTURE

Joining a new group can be intimidating. A welcoming ritual will offer the new student a sense of community as well as introduce the entire youth group to the spiritual practice of hospitality.

GETTING STARTED

You will need a small candle for each youth group member as well as paint markers. For the new student, use a white (or other light-colored) pillar candle.

THE RITUAL

Ask youth to sit in a circle, then invite them to reflect on what they enjoy about the youth group. Play some meditative background music. After a few minutes, invite them to decide on one word that characterizes the youth group. Then pass around the pillar candle and ask youth to write their words on the candle using the paint pens.

After everyone has added his or her word, give the new student the candle as a gift from the group and as a reminder that he or she is a member of this Christian community.

Next, invite youth to tell what they love about the youth group. Light the first person's candle, and ask him or her to point out something meaningful about the youth group. This person should then light the person's candle next to him or her and invite this youth to do the same. Continue the process around the circle.

After everyone has participated, allow youth to choose a special song to sing. Before singing, say the words aloud to emphasize the meaning. Then close by singing the song together.

79 A Ritual for the Untimely Loss of a Student

OPENING BLESSING
Step into our midst, Holy God.
Step into our pain and suffering.
Walk alongside us, Lord, and walk in our same heavy footsteps.

Step into our midst, Holy God.
Listen to our hurt, our feelings of loss, and see the absence in our hearts.

Step into our midst, Holy God.
Weave a great story that tells about this sacred life we have lost. Amen.

READINGS

How long, O LORD? Will you forget me forever?
How long will you hide your face from me?
How long must I bear pain in my soul,
    and have sorrow in my heart all day long?
How long shall my enemy be exalted over me?

Consider and answer me, O LORD my God!
Give light to my eyes, or I will sleep the sleep
    of death, and my enemy will say, "I have
prevailed"; my foes will rejoice because I am shaken.

But I trusted in your steadfast love;
My heart shall rejoice in your salvation.
I will sing to the Lord, because he has dealt bountifully
with me.

—Psalm 13:1-6

For I am convinced that neither death, nor life, nor
angels, nor rulers, nor things present, nor things to come,
nor powers, nor height, nor depth, nor anything else in
all creation, will be able to separate us from the love of
God in Christ Jesus our Lord.

—Romans 8:38-39

[Jesus said], "Remember, I am with you always, to the end
of the age."

—Matthew 28:20b

REMEMBERING
This is a time to tell stories, serve favorite snacks, sing or listen to meaningful songs, sit in silence, draw pictures, make cards, pray, meditate, or light candles. You decide the best way to remember the life of the student who has passed away.

CLOSING BLESSING

Into your hands, O God,

We all commit ourselves.

Into your presence, O God,

May we walk daily.

Beside us and all around us, O God,

May you be forever.

Help us to continue to tell the stories
that we have shared tonight,

**Keeping memories and friendships
alive forever. Amen.**

80 A Ritual for Advent: Watching and Waiting

THE BIG PICTURE

Advent is a wonderful tradition to begin in your youth group (if you don't already observe it). Advent is the season in the Christian tradition that leads up to Christmas. It means "coming" and is a time to prepare for the "coming" of Jesus. In this ritual, students will take a mini-pilgrimage to Bethlehem and sing songs that help prepare them for Christmas.

GETTING STARTED

You will need long strands of blue or purple fabric to create a "Prayer Path" (students will actually walk on the path). The path will have four stops: (1) The Entrance, (2) Angelic Choir, (3) Light in Darkness, and (4) Light to the World.

Collect the following supplies for use at the stops: song sheets for Christmas songs/hymns; one tall, purple pillar candle; a tea light candle for each student; and the following instructions for each "Stop":

  Stop 1: Poster with two questions
  Stop 2: Hymnals and song sheets
  Stop 3: Index card with question and Scripture
  Stop 4: Index card for each youth to take home with
         prayer and Scripture written on it

THE RITUAL

In this ritual the youth will take a journey along an "Advent Prayer Path." Before beginning the walk, divide the youth into small groups for "traveling."

Stop 1: The Entrance

Invite youth to take off their shoes while meditating on the following questions:

(1) Can you think of times that you had to wait on something that you were looking forward to?

(2) As you waited, how did you feel?

Stop 2: The Angelic Choir

In the story of Jesus' birth, angels sang songs of praise in a field where there were only shepherds and their flocks of sheep. As you prepare for Jesus' birth during this Advent season, think of things that will draw you closer to God, such as prayer, fasting, volunteering at a homeless shelter, and so on. Then, as a group, look through the song sheets and pick a hymn or chorus to sing together. While you are singing, imagine you are in the field with the shepherds on that cool starry night.

Stop 3: Light in Darkness

Place the purple pillar candle where youth can sit in front of it and meditate on this question:

Where in today's society are people sitting
in darkness and in need of a light?

"What came into existence was Life, and the Life was Light to live by. The Life-Light blazed out of the darkness; the darkness couldn't put it out." (John 1:3b-5, *THE MESSAGE*)

Stop 4: Light to the World

Give each student a tea light to take home and burn during this season of Advent. As youth focus on their candle flames, they should pray this prayer: "Lord Jesus, you give me light so I can be a light to others."

"Every person entering Life, he [Jesus] brings into Light." (John 1:9, *THE MESSAGE*)

81   A Ritual for the Body of Christ

THE BIG PICTURE

As the body of Christ, we are a community of people called to live our lives in a way that sets us apart from the world. Jesus commands and expects his followers to live together peaceably, setting an example for all those who watch.

In this ritual, youth will look at resources and reflect on ways they can be examples of peace and work for justice in the world.

GETTING STARTED

Cover a wall with large sheets of paper. In the middle of the wall and in large letters, write the words "Wall of Life." On a table, provide copies of current newspapers and culture-oriented magazines, along with scissors, glue, markers, and pieces of construction paper cut in the shapes of hands and feet.

THE RITUAL

Ask a student to read aloud Matthew 5:3-16. As the passage is read, ask youth to listen with their hearts and minds and to notice what images come to mind. Allow those who wish to tell about some of their images and thoughts.

When everyone has contributed, invite students to spend some time at the "Wall of Life." Tell them to look through the provided materials for images, words, or symbols representing life and unity. They should cut out the images (or words and symbols) and glue or tape them to a "hand" or "foot." Then the hands and feet should be posted on the "Wall of Life."

Close the time with this prayer:

Lord, we are your hands and feet in this world.
Help us to spread peace, unity, love, and grace. Amen.

Section 3
Guided
Meditations

82   A New Vision
Micah 5:2-5

PRAYER STATION

Set up a few prayer stations. At each one have
newspaper clippings and pictures that show
need: suffering, brokenness of the world,
poverty, disease, war, and so on. Set out clay,
paper, and markers for youth to sculpt, write,
or draw to express themselves during the guided
meditation. Invite them to sit around the stations in
small groups. Slowly read the meditation. You may want
to play some meditative music.

Meditation

*From the least likely of places God's chosen
comes . . . from the busy schedules of athletics, club
meetings, afterschool rehearsals, homework, relationships,
work, family commitments, and all of our life's
activities, God calls you—sometimes the least likely
candidate for God's work.
The world is hurting . . . The world is lost . . .
The world is broken.
(pause)
Focus on the images in front of you and imagine
God holding the world and all of its suffering in God's
hands. Now imagine that from God's hands springs a
new earth, a new vision of how the world ought to be.
What does it look like?
(pause)
Now hold that new vision in your hands.
How does it feel? What does it look like?
(pause)*

Just as God came in the form of Jesus to a hurting world,
God continues to come into the world through us.
Take the new vision that is in your hands and allow it to
enter your mind. Take the new vision that is in your
hands and in your mind and allow it to enter your heart.
Take the new vision that is in your hands, mind,
and heart, and ask God to send you into the world
to make the vision real.

83   Are We There Yet?
John 13:31-35

PRAYER STATION
Hang a large sheet of paper on the wall and invite youth
to spend several moments drawing symbols or words
that reflect how the world could be different if we loved
others the way Jesus loves us.

Meditation
What do you imagine Jesus' voice would sound like?
If Jesus were to say something to you, what would he say?
Imagine Jesus walking towards you. He looks at you
tenderly and says: "Where love is, I am.
So go and love others the way I have loved you."
Where would you go to show that
kind of love?
What does it feel like to love others the
same way Jesus loves you?
How would you be changed by
loving like Jesus does?

84 Following the Way of Christ

Romans 6:3-11

PRAYER STATION
You will need blue beads with holes in them and leather string. Invite youth to make "baptismal bead" bracelets. While making them, have them reflect on their baptisms and how being part of a community of faith shapes them.

Meditation

*The gills of a fish allow oxygen to pass into the
body and water to flow out, making it possible
for them to live under water.
Under the water there is life: a world both
foreign and familiar.
Remember your baptism—life—under the water . . .
a world both foreign and familiar.
That's what baptism means. You've acquired gills—
and are now a native in a new world: God's world.
Remember your baptism . . . learn to swim.
Jump out of the boat—the world—into the water.
Follow Christ into the deep end and into
deep places of prayer.
Remember your baptism. You are not the same.
You do not belong only to yourself. You are part of a
school of fish: all shapes and sizes,
different thoughts, beliefs, ideas, and abilities.
Remember your baptism—and swim!*

85   Get Behind Me
Mark 8:31-38

Meditation

Stop! Slow down! Take a breath.
Recall the events and activities that have filled your week
so far. How much of that time has been spent doing
something good for others? How much of that time has
been spent doing something for your personal gain?

Now imagine that you have arrived at a peaceful place.
As you are sitting and resting, Jesus approaches you.
He begins to name all the activities and events from your
week. He then looks deeply and intently into your eyes
and says, "Get behind me."

Now think again of your busy week. Only this time
imagine that you are following Jesus as he leads.
Have your activities and choices changed? Ask Jesus
if there is anything that you need to change about your
life in order to follow him.

Ask for guidance and courage to follow Jesus and the
direction he would lead you in life.

Get behind Jesus.

86   I Am Beyond
2 Samuel 7:1-11

PRAYER STATION

In the middle of a large sheet of paper, write the phrase *I Am Beyond* in large letters, then draw a circle around it. As a response to the reading, invite youth to add to the chart their descriptive words and phrases for God.

Meditation

Imagine you have walked for a long time, struggled up the side of a mountain, traveled through every weather element and season—all because you were searching for the ONE, the one ancients called "I AM"— the one the Christians called ABBA or DADDY.

Look out across the summit and wait in silence. Then you hear a voice, "Did you think that I live on this mountain? Or did you think that I live in a church? Or maybe you thought that I live in a book."

I am beyond . . .
I do not belong to you . . .
I am the One who created all that you see.
I belong to no one, but everything belongs to me.
I love everything that I created.

How does it feel to be in the presence of God? Has your perception of God changed by what you have heard?

87   *I'm Out of Control*
Psalm 146:3-6

PRAYER STATION

This meditation is a journaling exercise. Hand out paper and invite youth to record their thoughts and prayers as you read aloud the meditation. Pause between sections of the reading while students explore their feelings and thoughts. When you have finished, invite youth to tell "what happens next."

Meditation

"Do not put your trust in princes, in mortals, in whom there is no help." I depend too much on others. How did I get away with that? I'm out of control.

"Happy are those whose help is in the Lord their God." Lord, give me strength and wisdom concerning these issues in my life. I'm out of control, and I want you to be in control.

"God made heaven and the earth, the sea, and all that is in them." I am just part of your story, Lord, help me to see my place.

Imagine your life as though it were a story—God's story. Now imagine that God wants to share the next part of the story with you. What happens next?

88

Speed Trap
John 1:10-18

PRAYER STATION

Purchase some magnetic cards (at least one per student). Invite youth to create a "Speed Trap" magnet by writing the phrase *speed trap* on a card and then decorating it any way they choose.

Encourage them to take the magnets home or to school and position them in a prominent place so that when they see the magnets during the day, they are reminded to stop, relax, and say a short prayer.

Meditation

Everything moves so fast: homework, projects, grades, school, family, relationships, growing up, chores, fast food, college applications, sports, practices, band, dance, honor societies, make-up work, love, romance, pain, and so on.
(Continue the list using your life experiences.)

Everything seems to move in fast-forward motion;
it's almost as if we blink—and life has passed us by.
Scripture says that Jesus was in the world,
the world was there through him,
and yet the world didn't even notice.

It's almost as if we blinked—
and Jesus passed us by.

Now we have a world that is filled with fear, war,
suffering, hurt, stress, selfishness, greed . . .
(Continue the list from your life experiences.)

Scripture says that Jesus is still with us,
even until the end of time. He calls us to be his body
and to do his work in the world today.

Jesus is saying slow down; you've entered my speed trap.
Take a moment and relax . . . renew . . .
then respond.

Relax . . . listen to my words and let them sink deep
within you, deep into your heart. Then lock those words
where they cannot come out. Relax.

Renew . . . take those words and let them be words of
peace and healing for you. Let my words be strength
for the journey of life. Renew.

Respond . . . now go and live out the words you
have heard and felt. Be my living words.
Live my words. Respond.

Everything moves fast—
until you move into my "speed trap."

89 Life Together

Acts 2:1-21

PRAYER STATION

Hand out clay and have students mold symbols of how they think they fit into God's dream for creation. After sufficient time, invite youth to tell about their work.

Meditation

It's windy and there's a strong breeze—stronger than usual. I'm sitting among the trees, but not the kind of trees that grow in my backyard or in my neighborhood park. These trees are old—ancient even; they tell stories of long ago, only we've forgotten their language.

Today the trees are talking, and the wind is listening. I'm also listening, but I don't understand. Then I hear the faintest sound: a whisper, cold yet warm, breezy, and very gentle.

The wind is talking, and I begin to understand. The wind is telling me the story of the trees— a story of God's love that existed even before God's love for humans. God always had us in mind, but God's plan is so much bigger. The wind is a part of God's plan, along with these trees, and humanity, and even me. Where do I fit into God's dream for creation?

Worship Feast: Readings

90   Enter At Your Own Risk

Mark 1:4-11

PRAYER STATION

In the middle of the room, arrange several bowls of water
and a container of soil. Invite students to come and scoop
up a handful of soil, then reflect upon the ways they feel
distant from God. Next tell them to wash their hands in a
bowl of water. As they wash their hands, encourage
youth to reflect on what they need to change in their
lives in order to draw closer to God.

Meditation

*In the wilderness we meet strange figures . . .
undomesticated and mad, saying to us:
"You can change. You must change."*

*Come to the desert and hear the prophet proclaim:
"You can change. You must change!"*

*What do you need to change about yourself
in order to draw closer to God?*

91

The Desert
Luke 4:1-3

PRAYER STATION

Create a "desert space." Use tarps or flat containers of sand. Place stones or rocks in the sand for students to use during the meditation. Encourage students to allow their minds to wander freely and give them a few minutes to experience silence.

Meditation

The desert is dry, sometimes very hot, stale, and dead—sometimes cold, lonely, and dark.

Walk into the desert as Jesus did: alone, taking nothing with you except your thoughts, fears, and questions.

Being alone can do strange things to your mind. Take a deep breath, then allow your imagination to wander freely through the desert of your thoughts.

Imagine yourself in the desert. You hear a voice calling your name. You follow this voice to the top of a large dune. Once you are at the top of the dune, you find a small rock. Hold the rock in your hand.
The rock represents the things in life that tempt you to turn away from your life with God. As you look at the rock, imagine that you see yourself within the rock, tempted to be something that you are not.

Worship Feast: Readings

Now you hear another voice,
different from the voice you've heard before.
You recognize it; it is the voice of the Christ.
He is asking you: "Do you know who you are? Tell me."

Now look at the rock and imagine yourself as only you can
see. Tell the Christ who you are: the you that is free from
labels, stress, and expectations.

Ask Jesus for strength to live more fully as the "real" you.
Then carry your rock with you out of the desert as a
reminder of what you have witnessed.

92   Forgiveness
Matthew 18:23-35

PRAYER STATION
Have youth paraphrase Matthew 18:23-35, or invite them
to create their own stories about forgiveness.

Meditation
Is forgiveness the way Jesus explains it really all that
practical? Do I have to forgive someone who hurts me
over and over? What about me? Who in my life do I
continually hurt, even though I'm unaware
or it's unintentional?

Forgiveness is another chance at friendship—
another chance to love—
another chance to make things right.
Forgiveness is the way of Christ—
and the way of you and me as
his followers.

93 We Are in God's Image

Isaiah 11:1-10

PRAYER STATION

Set up some mirrors around your room. As you read the meditation, invite youth to look into a mirror.

Meditation

Out of the ground we come. . . each of us, different and wonderful in our own way. Out of heaven God comes . . . looking for a people to call God's own, a people to be shaped and formed in God's own image: loving, wise, compassionate, and peaceful.

These people—the people of God—are you and me. We come in all colors, with different ways of seeing our Creator. Sometimes we agree, and sometimes we don't. But we come together as the body, praising God.

We—the people in God's image—live side by side, loving one another, even when it is hard to love. Who is it hard to love right now?

We—the people of God's image— eat alongside those who have nothing, sharing what we have. Who in this life is in need of something that you can share?

We—the people of God's image—
are called to be an example for the whole world
of how to live life together.
How do we do that here and now?

We are the people of God's image.
Look into the mirror. What do you see?

You . . . You are . . .
You are a person of God's image . . .
What do you see?

94   Beloved

Psalm 112:1-10

PRAYER STATION

Display a variety of mirrors in the prayer station and invite students to spend time imagining how God sees them rather than how they see themselves.

Meditation

A sunrise, breaking through the night . . .
Compassion like a well that never runs dry . . .

God's grace . . . showers God's beloved.

You are God's beloved child—
a wonderful creation,
beautiful and exquisite.
You are God's beloved child—
like a sunrise, like a well that
never runs dry.

95 God's Retreat House
Psalm 71:1-6

Meditation

I'm running on empty. I simply don't know when to slow down. Help me to slow down. I'm up to my neck in stress. I have so many things going on that I feel like I might just shut down.

Imagine you're walking along, carrying a bag filled with all the events and activities of your life. Feel the weight of the bag and look at its size.

Now look into the distance. Do you see someone coming toward you? As he moves closer, you recognize him as Jesus the Christ. By this time, you are exhausted from holding the heavy bag of your life.

Jesus looks into your eyes and says, "I want you to put down the bag for a while, then turn around and look." It feels so good to put down the bag. You turn around just as Jesus said. You see a large, very inviting house. Jesus says: "I've been waiting for you. This house is a place of rest and peace. Come in and experience the wonderful love that you can find only in this house.

As you sit in God's retreat house, reflect upon how it feels to know there is a place where you can lay down your life and experience peace.

96   If He Calls, Say "Yes!"
Matthew 4:12-23

PRAYER STATION

After reading aloud the meditation, invite students to respond to one of Jesus' requests in the meditation by writing him either an e-mail or a text message.

Meditation

If Jesus called you today, what would you say to him?
What would you like to ask him?

If Jesus called you today and
needed you to help someone,
who in your life might he be asking you to help?

If Jesus called you today and asked you
to forgive someone for hurting you,
who might he be asking you to forgive?

If Jesus called you today
and asked you to follow him,
where would he take you?

97 Love Makes the World Go Around

Proverbs 31:10–31

PRAYER STATION

Write the words *Love Is* . . . on a large sheet of paper, then hang it on the wall. Invite students to draw or write words, images, or poems to express what they believe to be the true meaning of love.

Meditation

Love is hard to find sometimes—
And other times it's just around the corner.

Love goes out of it's way . . .
Love shows up at unexpected times with cute surprises
that turn a bad day into a better day.
Love is like beautiful music,
inspirational when played well.
Love shows up in both surprising ways and
in routine ways.
Love is a gift that transcends . . .
a gift that comes from God.

98 Nothing Is Working the Way I Planned

Luke 6:17-26

PRAYER STATION

Provide stationery and pencils and invite students to write letters to Jesus. Encourage them to tell him anything that's on their minds.

Meditation

Sometimes life takes a turn for the worse and there's one cloudy day after another. In what ways has your life seemed cloudy lately?

Jesus said, "You're blessed when you've lost it all. God's kingdom is there for the finding." What does God's kingdom look like to you?

Sometimes we feel empty inside, like nothing we do is going to get us through the day. Jesus said, "You're blessed when you're ravenously hungry. Then you're ready for the messianic meal." What does this meal taste like?

Sometimes it seems like everyone gangs up on you and no one understands who you are.

Jesus said, "Count yourself blessed every time people put you down or throw you out. . . What it means is that the truth is too close for comfort and they are uncomfortable." (Matthew 5:11, THE MESSAGE)

99 Speaking a Word
Luke 10:1-11, 16-20

PRAYER STATION
Hand out modeling clay and invite students to play with the clay as you read aloud the meditation. Afterwards, invite youth to mold the clay into a symbol or expression of God's peace.

Meditation
Imagine that you are one of the twelve disciples.
Where might Jesus send you?
What would it be like to travel on foot to
your destination? How would it feel to know that you
can take nothing with you?
What would you miss?

Jesus has told you that when you enter a city you must tell
people that "the kingdom of God is near."
How would you express this truth?
How do you picture the kingdom of God?

Jesus told his disciples that when they entered a home they
should greet the family with a sign of peace.
Where do you need peace right now?
Where might you be able to show
someone a sign of peace?

100

Wake Up!
Mark 16:1-8

PRAYER STATION

Invite youth to look through newspapers for glimpses of Jesus, then cut out the images and stories to create a "Resurrection Collage."

Meditation

The stone has been moved . . . rolled back. Look inside.
What do you see? Do you hear a voice?
"The one you are looking for is not here.
He was, but he's gone now."

Don't look in the place of the dead to find
the ultimate expression of life.
Jesus is alive, not in the tomb but all around us.

Where do you see glimpses of Jesus
in the world? Where do you see
love, understanding, justice, and mercy?

Worship Feast Resources

❋ *Worship Feast Services: 50 Complete Multi-Sensory Services for Youth.* This comprehensive resource includes services for the various seasons, prayer and healing, discovering your spiritual type, graduates, and many more. ISBN: 0687063671.

❋ *Worship Feast Ideas: 100 Awesome Ideas for Postmodern Youth.* This resource includes ideas for creating your own services or incorporating multisensory worship elements into your existing services. ISBN: 0687063574.

❋ *Worship Feast Dramas: 15 Sketches for Youth Groups, Worship, & More,* by Beth Miller. This resource provides a variety of long and short skits that ask serious questions about maintaining a life of faith in a not-so-faith-friendly world. ISBN: 0687044596.

❋ *Worship Feast Taizé: 20 Complete Services in the Spirit of Taizé* with CD-Rom, by Jenny Youngman. This resource includes services that offer meditations, song suggestions, prayers, and silence. Includes a split-track music CD with options for singing voice only, instrumental only, or both voices and instruments. ISBN: 068774192

❋ *Worship Feast Taizé Songbook.* A companion piece for *Worship Feast: 20 Complete Services,* this resource includes fifteen popular and easy-to-sing Taizé songs that will lead youth and youth workers to a deeper prayer experience. ISBN: 0687739322.